Shouting in the Darkness

FAITH-FILLED POEMS TO ENCOURAGE AND INSPIRE

*"I know you and I chose you,
you are who you're meant to be.
When I look at you I look with love,
it is my child that I see."*

Elizabeth Rushmer

Shouting in the Darkness
by Elizabeth Rushmer.

First published 2022.

Copyright © Elizabeth Rushmer 2022.

Cover by Red Axe Design.

Book interior by Eleanor Abraham.

Interior illustrations by m0leks, cgterminal
and Alexander_P, courtesy of Shutterstock;
and by milalala, vectortatu and Mokographic,
courtesy of iStock.

Typeset in Bodoni URW.

ISBN: 9798840812082

Contents

Shouting in the darkness

I was shouting in the darkness.
No one heard. I was on my own.
I couldn't get much lower,
I was lost and all alone.
But you heard my pain as I cried out
and immediately came to me.
'Take my hand. I can save your life.
'I will set you free,'
are the words I heard you say.
But still I was unsure.
Surely it wasn't that simple?
Surely there'd be more?
But still I felt I had no choice,
I was stuck there on my own.
All you wanted was my love
and to have me as your own.
I still have scars and scrapes and bruises
from how things used to be,
but with you I'm slowly healing
and becoming who I'm meant to be.

Haunted eyes

You search for me with those haunted
    eyes,
no longer able to distinguish between
    truth and lies,
abandoned by all you've known and
    loved,
you've reached the end, you've had
    enough.
But because you search I'll make myself
    known.
I'll show the way, I'll guide you home.
No one is rejected if they sincerely ask.
Now you're in my presence, you can
    remove your mask.

Hear your voice

You call out to me and I hear your voice,
I can hear your words through your pain.
Keep on believing that I am here,
I will heal your hurt and remove your
　　shame.
You aren't alone as you began to think,
I would never ever leave your side.
There's nowhere you can go without me,
there's nowhere you could ever hide.
So pour it all out, though I already know,
Say what's on your heart with honesty,
There's nothing you can say that I don't
　　know,
I want to help you and set you free.

I wasn't designed to go it alone

I wasn't designed to go it alone,
I can't manage this life all on my own.
But that's not the way it has to be –
you promise you'll walk each step with me.
You want to guide me and keep me safe,
invite me in to your loving embrace.
You make it simple, no need to guess,
all I need is to believe and say yes.

I don't understand

I don't understand,
the tears continue to flow,
I keep asking why
but I'll never know.
I'm lost, set adrift,
can't think what to do,
so I reach out both hands
and cling tightly to you.

Part the clouds

Part the clouds and let the sun shine through,
stop the storm I plead with you.
Quiet the noise, I need it to cease –
no more turmoil. I need your peace.
Save me from this pain inside.
Build me up so I need no longer hide.
You know the troubles that burden me,
there's nothing in my life that you don't see.
I call out in tears and put my hope in you.
I need your help, I don't know what to do.

After the clouds

After the clouds and the storm fades away,
once the darkness has lifted and the light finds
    its way,
I can appreciate the calm because I made it
    through.
I can think on what happened and reflect on
    what's true.
I can start to make changes once I see what was
    wrong.
I can put it behind me and start to move on.
I can learn from mistakes, I'll be stronger next
    time.
I'll keep moving forward, your hand in mine.

You don't give up on me

You don't give up on me
no matter how far I fall.
I can't hide my faults from you
you always know it all.
Despite knowing me completely,
your love is an endless supply.
I'm so grateful that you offer it,
on your unfailing love I rely.
It's too wondrous to think
of all that you've given to me.
You found me and saved me.
You healed me, set me free.
So I thank you and I praise you
for all that you have done.
I give myself to you –
this heart you have won.

Too much to bear

The worry and pain was too much
    to bear
so I buried it way down deep.
Though others tried to help me
nothing could bring relief.
So at my lowest I cried out to God
to heal me and help me forgive.
With joy and tears I received his
    blessing.
He freed me so I could live.

Wash me clean

Wash me clean from what's gone before,
renew my spirit, release my pain.
All my hope I put in you,
you bring freedom and break every chain.
Help me wholeheartedly search for you,
and not be distracted in my days.
With you I know I can endure –
I trust in you and all your ways.

Make me new

Clean me up and make me new
do the things you need to do.
Scrape away and polish me up,
refill me from your flowing cup.
Alone I stand – incomplete,
I need your hand to guide my feet,
to light my way and make it clear,
to stand with me when I'm struck
   with fear.
You alone can help me through,
you alone know what to do.

Speak peace into my life

Speak peace into my life –
Help me find the calm within the storm.
Today it seems that busyness
and rushing is the norm.
Help me clear away the excess
and get rid of what shouldn't be mine.
Help me consciously choose the way I
    live
and more wisely use my time.

I wonder

You draw me in and I wonder
how I ever could not have known,
that there was a much better way
than trying to live life on my own.
You loved me when I was ignorant
of all I had to gain,
and you waited patiently for me
to realise my need and call out your
    name.
You don't blame me for keeping
    you waiting
you're just happy that I am here.
And now that I have found you
I'm going to keep you near.

I chose you

I know you and I chose you,
you are who you're meant to be.
When I look at you I look with love,
it is my child that I see.
You are enough so please let go
of what already has been forgiven.
I don't want you to stay in bondage
but to follow me and start living.

Heal the hurts

Heal the hurts inside of me,
release the pain and set me free.
Light my way so I can see.
Lead me to who I ought to be.
I can't do this on my own –
open my mind and help me grow.
Send me out, your seeds to sow
so that all around will come to
    know.

I can't even get the words out

Sometimes I can't even get the words out
and you just comfort me when I cry.
You listen to my confusion and
    complaints
as I try to find an answer to "why".
You're with me in my time of need
and you set me on the right path.
No concern is too small for you –
you always help me when I ask.

Out of my depth

I'm out of my depth, can't see a way
    through,
I don't understand so I'm looking to you.
Make clear the decision you want me to
    make.
Show me the path you want me to take.
If left to myself I'll just struggle along
but if you guide my steps I won't get it
    wrong.

Wake in the darkness

You wake in the darkness
calling out my name.
I'm already at your side
to soothe away your pain.
Tired and confused,
you don't need to explain.
I will stay and hold you close
until you're at peace again.

Face up to my failings

You help me face up to my failings
and the cleansing tears flow.
I confess to all my wrongdoing
though there's nothing you don't
    know.
But you don't leave me in this place.
Once dealt with, you set me free,
no longer burdened by my past.
You help me become a better me.

Calm my mind

Calm my mind and still my emotions,
let the tension within find release.
Help me step away from my problems
and find my way into your peace.
I can't think clearly when I'm tense
    and worried,
help me pause and start to breathe.
Give me your wisdom to see things
    clearly
when I look to you my mind is freed.

Today was too hard

Today was too hard and too painful,
nothing went according to plan.
It's drained me of all of my strength,
it's tested all that I am.
I'm down but I won't be disheartened,
I'll let go and find refreshment in you.
I'll go to sleep safe in the knowledge,
that you make each and every day
    new.

Don't let them steal your smile

Please don't let them steal your smile
no matter how much it hurts inside.
They're just trying to cause you pain –
to make you curl up and hide.
You're worth so much more than you think.
You're just how you're meant to be,
and until you learn to fully love yourself
I'll keep topping you up with love from me.

Self-criticism

I won't listen to self-criticism
or doubts forming in my mind.
If I start off down that dangerous road
it's only destruction that I'll find.
Instead, I'll turn my thoughts to you,
so you can remind me who I am.
I'm your child, I'm greatly loved,
I'm part of your amazing plan.

Leave your bags with me

Leave your bags with me,
just place them down,
you no longer need
to carry them around.
They're much too heavy
and to hard to bear,
please listen to me,
just leave them there.
If you take them along
you won't manage your task.
Just trust in me
it's all I ask.
I'll give you the strength
to climb that hill.
Let go of your baggage
so you're free to do my will.

Wander around the wilderness

Don't let me wander around the wilderness
but help me to face up to my fears.
I don't want to be haunted by past mistakes
or keep repeating them in coming years.
Make me brave enough to take a stand
and finally break away –
to let go of all that I once was
and walk with you each day.

Joys and troubles

Speak to me of your joys and troubles –
don't hold back, I want to know.
Explain to me your deep frustrations –
talk to me about every high and low.
You don't need fancy words to reach me –
I'm your loving father – just relax.
I'm ready to listen at any moment,
I'm always with you, please don't forget
    that.

Healed to live

You will be healed to live your life
and praise my holy name.
Though times are hard I'll see you
    through –
you'll be stronger, no longer the same.
I love you, my child, I'll keep you safe,
I'm holding you in my hand.
Keep the faith and trust in me,
so much more for you is planned.

Look to me for your answers

Look to me for your answers,
take your strength from my word.
Trust in me, I keep my promises,
nothing you say goes unheard.

Time to let go

It's time to let go of the resentment inside,
to no longer cling to my wounded pride.
When I go to sleep, start the next day anew,
and release old hurts that are clouding my
    view,
I shouldn't be critical of what others do,
but look beyond my thoughts and search for
    what's true.

Deep breath

Take a deep breath and count to ten,
pause and think before you start again.
Is it really worth it what you plan to
    say?
Could you phrase it in a better way?
Should you stop and just let it go?
Would it help to not let your feelings
    show?
You might be right but are you being
    loving?
Would it be better if you just said
    nothing?

You fought for me

You fought for me
when no one else would.
You paid the price
when no one else could.
You chased me down
and wouldn't leave my side.
You were with me in the darkness,
though I tried to hide.
You opened my eyes
to your love, goodness and grace.
I rejoice that you saved me
and offer me your embrace.

Take this burden

Let me take this burden from you,
there's nothing left that you can do.
You've tried your best, now let it go,
I'm doing things that you don't know.
Have faith in me, I'll sort your problem,
just sit back and await the outcome.

I'm good enough

I'm not perfect but I'm good enough.
Doing something is better than staying
    afraid.
Yes, I'll mess up but I'll keep on trying,
always aiming to follow the plan God
    made.
If others criticise I'll ignore them,
they don't really know what I'm trying to
    do.
I'm just doing my best to listen
and respond to the words that come from
    you.

Faith not feelings

Trust in your faith not in your
    feelings.
Trust in the promises that you've
    been given.
Trust in the word that you are
    reading –
use it to guide how you are living.

I thought I was nothing

When I thought I was nothing
you knew who I was.
When I couldn't find my way,
you had a plan.
When I was focused on myself
you drew me to others.
You keep returning me to you,
the great I Am.

Help me be more

Lord help me be more than I currently am,
I don't feel qualified to carry out your plan.
The things you ask just feel too tough,
I'm not sure who I am will be enough.
But the doubts I have are only in me,
and I trust in you to provide all that I need.
If you've asked me to do it you'll make a way,
so I'll follow your prompting and do as you
    say.

Deceived by the voice

Deceived by the voice
that keeps speaking your name,
don't get drawn in,
condemnation's his game –
trying to make you think
all hope is gone,
that there's no point in trying,
no going on.
But you've been granted forgiveness,
your conscience is clear.
So it's time to call him out,
it's not your own thoughts you hear.
There's no point rethinking it,
it's time to let go.
Turn away from that voice
and towards the truth that you know.

Stay away from the darkness

Stay away from the darkness
you won't find your answers
   there,
that way only leads to misery
to anguish and despair.
It'll try to trick you into
   believing
it'll give you the desires of your
   heart.
When really its aim is to kill and
   destroy
and to tear your life apart.

Draw me in

Draw me in to your embrace
I long to hide in your safe space.
I'm feeling weary and long for rest,
I feel I've failed every test.
But in your presence I feel renewed
and all I ask is that you would
give me strength for what comes my way
and refresh me for the coming day.

What you have

Come to me with what you have,
that's enough for me.
I know the story of your past
and how you came to be.
There's nothing you can surprise
    me with
so lay your troubles down,
confess your faults, let's start again
and turn your life around.

I wish I could

I wish I could take away your worries
and help you deal with the pain.
I wish I could remove your burdens
and help you to smile again.
But all I can do is offer support
and for your needs I'll continue to
    pray,
and I'll guide you to the only one
who is able to show you the way.

Call to me

Call to me in the quiet places,
seek me when you're tired.
Turn to me when you're worn out
and you no longer feel inspired.
I know you're only human
and your emotions ebb and flow,
but I remain unchanging,
so trust in what you know.
Focus on me in the hard times,
when life feels so unfair.
I am your hope for the future
I've already planned out your share
of good things, of prosperity,
of time spent on the mountain top.
But to get there you can't give up –
keep believing, never stop.

We need you

We need your help, we need you here,
the pain and suffering is all too clear.
On our own we won't get through.
Without your guidance what can we
    do?
So come to us, be with us now.
We want to help – show us how.

I lift my eyes

I lift my eyes up to the hills –
the journey will be long and hard
   for me.
The path appears and disappears
extending as far as I can see.
You're calling me to meet with you,
I walk and I will not stop.
Your voice keeps telling me to
   come,
I'll meet you at the mountain top.

Set you free

I am with you and want to set you free.
My plan is for you to live abundantly.
I want you to achieve all you can in life,
regardless of your past mistakes and
    strife.
So turn to me and let go of the past –
follow my guidance and do as I ask.
You'll find peace and joy when you do my
    will –
taste the living waters and drink your fill.

Turn the light on

Turn the light on, make all things
    clear,
help me understand what it is I
    hear.
Without your revelation there is no
    hope –
without your insight it's too hard to
    cope.
How in the world can people get by
if only on themselves do they
    choose to rely?

Strongholds in me

Open my eyes to the strongholds in me,
I trust you, Lord, to set me free.
Show me where I need to change,
my whole life I will rearrange.
All things are possible if I'm in it with
    you.
I know you're faithful and your promises
    are true.
Day by day you help me grow,
I thank you, Lord, that you love me so.

Chip away

Chip away at me until you shine
  through.
Chip away at me until I'm made
  new.
I believe that you reside within me
but it'll take work until that's clear
  to see.
I'll work with you and I won't give
  up
until I love others as you love us.

Trust in me

Trust in me that's all I ask
and let me have my say.
Stop being busy making plans,
it's better done my way.
I know the plans I have for you
so trust in me, I ask,
you know that I am faithful
and will help you in your task.
Be prepared to wait on me
until the time is right,
I am always here for you,
I'm never out of sight.

The little things

I'm interested in the little things –
all that that happens to you every day.
Though I already know it all
I long to hear you what you have to
    say.
Tell me what you're up to
and ask me to be with you,
say what it is you're worried about
and ask me to help you through.
Tell me that you're grateful –
thank me for everything I provide.
Tell me that you feel my presence,
that you know I'm at your side.
Don't speak to me in fancy words,
that isn't what I desire,
just come to me with a humble heart,
your love is all I require.

Wounded heart

Lord heal this wounded heart of mine,
I've wept so many tears.
I keep trying to move forwards
but take steps back throughout the years.
I cry out to you in anguish,
knowing only you can heal my pain.
Please show me how things can be better,
I don't want my life to stay the same.

I'll change things

Please ask and I'll help when you can't
    manage.
I'll change things when you're stuck
    where you're at.
Don't worry about the size of your
    problem
bring it to me and I'll say 'I'll handle
    that'.
It might not be how you'd expect it
and it may take longer than you'd like.
But have faith that I'm working for your
    good
and I'm right beside you in your fight.

I can't fully comprehend

I can't fully comprehend
why you'd do such a thing for me.
You sacrificed your son
so I could be set free.
Surely I can't be worth it,
with all my faults and sin.
But to you I am – you opened your arms
and welcomed me right in.
So while I can't understand it,
I'm so grateful that it's true,
and that you had a plan
to bring me back to you.

Brick by brick

Brick by brick you took the wall down,
reordered my thoughts, turned my life
   around.
I praise you, Lord, for the work done
   in me,
once focused inward there's much
   more I now see.
Keep guiding and strengthening me
   throughout my days,
I long to know you better and grow in
   your ways.

Grow in love

Help me grow in your perfect love
I feel I've got so far to go –
if I've only myself to rely on
I won't have much to show.
Your command, it sounds so simple,
'Love God and your neighbour too'.
This is all that I want to achieve
but, in reality, it's so hard to do.
So fill me up with your love –
give me a love that I can share.
Help me to use it wisely,
help me to love and care.

My God is so good

My God is so good
he managed to change me,
he's raising me up
and others can see.
So I'll speak of his greatness
and won't be ashamed.
When I'm asked what's my
    secret,
it's God who'll be named.

Patient in the waiting

Help me be patient in the waiting.
I always feel that things take too long.
Help me stick to the plan you gave me
and not try to hurry things along.
I know you have your reasons
for doing things the way you do,
so help me stand firm while I'm enduring
and keep my eyes on you.

A light so others may see

Help me ensure that others feel heard.
Help me to not want to have the last
 word.
Help me not look down on others I see.
Help me be the best that I'm able to be.
Help me let go, to forgive and forget.
Help me leave others so they feel pleased
 that we met.
Help me treat others with the care you
 give me.
Help me be a light so others may see.

I can see you working

Thank you – I can see you working
and I know you want what's best for me.
Help me grow in faith and wisdom
as I wait on you patiently.
Sometimes it's clear what your plan is,
and sometimes I haven't a clue,
but each day if I remain in your presence
step by step you'll guide me through.

Cleansing fire

Let your cleansing fire fall on me,
burn off every fault and impurity.
Rebuild me, heal me, make me whole,
refresh my spirit, renew my soul.
I was broken but you can fix me.
I was in bondage but you set me free.

Always there

Always faithful through it all.
Always there to hear my call.
Always there to comfort me.
Always there to help me see.
Always there to correct my
    ways.
Always there to guide my
    days.
Always there to bring me
    peace.
Always there with a love that
    won't cease.

I miss the signs

I'm sorry that I miss the signs
that you put in front of me,
I'm so caught up in myself
I can't always clearly see.
You want me to put others first
but I find it hard to do,
I can't rely on myself
so I need to look to you.
Please guide me where I can help
with little gifts of love,
to introduce those in need
to the God of heaven above.

I can't change the way things are

I don't know what you're going through,
but I can hear the pain in your voice.
I wish I could stop you having to deal
    with it
but it seems you have no choice.
Unfortunately I can't change the way
    things are,
you won't get any great wisdom from me,
but I'll always be there to give you a hug
and listen to you over cake and coffee.

Despite the chaos

Despite the chaos all around
I can still see your light shine.
Though it's easy to feel afraid
I'm not when your hand's in mine.
Because of you, I still feel peace
during these troubled times.
I won't focus on the conflicts
it's still your truths I'll look to find.
I won't let my mind be distracted
by every negative voice.
Instead your presence and your love
will always be my choice.

Tension in my spirit

There's a tension in my spirit,
an unease about my soul.
I need to reconnect with you,
only you can make me whole.
Draw me close and show me
how it's meant to be.
I no longer want to seek out
what the world has for me.
It cannot provide me
with what I really need.
Only you'll fulfil me –
with you I can succeed.

Quiet place

It's time to retreat to my quiet
    place,
to welcome your presence, to look
    on your face.
I want to discuss what's happened
    in my day
and I want to listen to what you
    have to say.
When I'm with you I can feel your
    peace,
I can start to relax and let my
    tensions release.
Though my problems remain, you
    help me see a way through,
when you're in it with me there's
    nothing I can't do.

Sit in peace

Help me, Lord, just to sit in peace,
to not have restless hands or feet,
to not always be thinking of things
    to do,
but to relax in silence and wait on
    you.
I ask for help and tell you each
    concern,
but if I'm not quiet how can I learn
what your answer is or what you
    plan to do?
I won't learn much if I don't listen
    to you.

Enter your presence

Let me enter your presence
and receive my fill.
Let me listen in silence
and hear your will.
Let me wait expectantly
for what may be heard.
Let me find peace and joy
in absorbing your word.

Lift the burdens

Lift the burdens that weigh me down,
help me turn my life around.
I see what it is I have to do
but I'm helpless to do it without you.
Only you can give me the strength I
    need.
Only with you can I be freed.

Showing me what's right

Thank you, Lord, for showing me what's
    right
when you see me getting it wrong.
Thank you, Lord, for turning my sorrow
into a joyful song.
Thank you, Lord, for reaching out
when I feel lost and alone in the dark.
Thank you, Lord, for reigniting my fire
with your holy spark.

You refresh me

It's unrealistic to hope for no distractions
there are always things I must do.
But help me to carve out some quiet time
where I can spend it only with you.
I need to meet with you – you refresh
    me.
Your peace and your love bring me rest.
I need you to inspire and teach me,
so for others I'll be at my best.

Forgive me for my foolishness

Forgive me for my foolishness
when I forget the way –
when I choose unwisely
how I spend my day.
Awaken me once again
to your unfailing love,
help me keep my eyes on you
knowing you're enough.
Teach me to filter out
all that draws me from your side,
to be open and confess
rather than try and hide.
I know I have a long way to go
and won't always get things right,
but I'm moving in the best
    direction
when I keep you in my sight.

Why is it so hard?

Why is it so hard
to react the right way?
Why can't I keep quiet
and consider what to say?
Each day it's the same,
I don't seem to progress –
my annoyance remains
not seeming to get less.
So I'll confess each night
that today I got it wrong
and pray yet again
that tomorrow I'll be strong.
So come the next day
I might actually find
I've finally learnt
how to be patient and kind.

Show love to others

I'm determined to show love to others
in the same way God keeps loving me.
I'll choose it despite what's happening
even when it doesn't come naturally.
I might not feel it in my head,
but I don't have to act on how I feel.
So I'll make myself live in love
until it becomes part of me and real.

Small lit candle

Like a small lit candle flickering
I can only shine light around me,
but if we all burn brightly together
oh, how much further we will see.
On our own we're just not able
to reach out to everyone.
But if we all do what we do best,
we can achieve what needs to be done.

Comfortable and predictable

Only the comfortable and predictable
is where I like to be –
to know in advance how I'll respond,
and what's expected of me.
But I can't reach out to others
if I stay in my comfort zone,
so please help me to be brave –
I can't do this on my own.

Thoughts of you

Fill my mind with thoughts of you,
show me the things you would have me
    do.
Lead me in the way that's right.
Help me keep you in my sight.
Help me forgive and seek forgiveness –
to be humble and acknowledge my
    weakness,
to not make excuses for what I won't do,
but when I'm afraid to find courage in
    you.

I gave in too easily

I gave in too easily,
I didn't try and fight.
Now I'm ashamed –
trying to run from your sight.
But there's no place to go
where I could escape from you,
so what can I say,
what can I do?
But you welcome me back
with arms open wide.
You didn't want my silence,
there was no need to hide.
If I just come to you
and ask you to forgive
you'll release me from my
    burdens
so I'm free again to live.

Nothing's more important

Nothing's more important
than the time I spend with you,
especially if I'm doing
the things you ask me to.
I need to stay in your presence
to keep me right on track,
and if I veer from your instructions
I need to hear you call me back.

Do not be disheartened

Do not be disheartened by the delay.
I have a plan – keep doing it my way.
You're much too impatient, these things
    take time.
Don't look to your own strength, keep
    using mine.
I've asked you to do this, you're not
    doing it alone,
I'll always be with you, you're not on your
    own.

This world is changing

This world is changing
and it doesn't look good,
so many people
not acting how they should.
It's not always easy
to see who's wrong or right,
there are so many shades
between black and white.
I can't figure it all out
but I'll put my trust in you
and keep on doing
the things you want me to.
Though I find it hard
with ever-changing situations,
in you I find my rest –
you are my firm foundation.

Prepare me and inspire me

Prepare me and inspire me –
light a fire in my heart.
Get me ready for your calling,
I'm eager to start.
Point me in the direction
of where I ought to be.
I'm not sure where I'll end up
but I'm excited to see.

Stand firm in
my faith

I will stand firm in my faith
and keep my eyes on you.
Your promises still stand –
your words all hold true.
I refuse to give up
or allow doubts to take hold.
For I know you stand with me
in days of darkness and cold.

Stir in me a hunger

Stir in me a hunger
to seek until I find.
Give me a determination
for renewing of my mind.
Fill me with a need
to look beyond myself.
Ignite in me a passion
to be with you above all else.

My obedience

You asked for my obedience
and you told me what to do.
You were with me every step of the way
and helped me see it through.
Throughout the process I was confident
and at peace it would succeed.
because it was not my idea but yours,
you gave me everything I'd need.

If you ask

If you ask me to do it
then it shall be done.
If you ask me to fight for it
it shall be won.
If it's part of your plan
then that's how it should be.
If you need a willing helper
please look to me.
I may not be qualified
or be the best at the task,
but I offer my obedience
for whatever you ask.
I don't have great confidence
in my own individual skill
but I can achieve anything
if that is your will.

Time to meet

I need to take time to meet you more often,
to pause my activities and make my rushing cease.
It's only when I stop and settle in your presence
that I can hear what you say and welcome your
    peace.
There's a time and a place for busyness and doing,
few have the opportunity to spend all day in
    prayer.
But I know that I need to make time every day
to create some space and just meet with you there.

Build others up

Help me, Lord, to build others up,
to convince and not to condemn.
Each of us has so many faults
and we're not always aware of them.
You treat us gently and guide us with care
please teach us to act just the same,
so that others can feel when we speak
that we are sharing love in your name.

Show me you're interested

Show me you're interested
by coming to talk to me.
Don't just bring a shopping list
of the things you'd like to see.
Don't wait to seek me out
until you have a problem.
If you seek my guidance daily
I can help you avoid them.
I want us to talk
not because you should do
but because your love for me
makes you always want to.

Your body is a temple

Your body is a temple,
you should treat it with respect,
while you worship with your mind
there's more that I expect.
Keep yourself fit and healthy
there's work I need from you.
If you're not able when I ask
what are you going to do?
I live in that body with you,
so treat it with great care,
otherwise you'll reach the point
when it's damaged beyond repair.

Your sacrifice

I can't believe your sacrifice –
you gave your life for me.
Something that will be celebrated
for all eternity.
You spent your time amongst us,
focused on the task God gave to you
and despite all the opposition
you let God's love flow through.
I thank you for all the suffering
that you willingly took for me.
I thank you that your selfless act
meant that I could be set free.

Take thoughts captive

Help me take my thoughts captive so I can be
    free
of all the self doubt and fear that keeps welling
    up in me.
Help me not to believe any of the lies,
to be ready to fight back when the devil tries
to tell me I'm not worthy and that I'll never be
    any good.
Because I am. I've been washed by the blood.
I've been made righteous in Jesus's name.
I need no longer be weighed down by
    condemnation and shame.

Don't cry for me

Wipe your tears, don't cry for me,
I've gone beyond what the eye can see.
I'm at peace but I'm not alone.
I'm with the saints, I've made it home.

Your faithfulness

Thank you for your faithfulness
and your guidance every day.
You help me continue growing
and not get lost along the way.
The world brings its distractions
with things less important than
    they appear.
The answer is to listen
to your word and keep you near.

Break it to me gently

Break it to me gently
the error of my way.
All I need to do is ask
then listen to what you say.
You tell me that you love me,
followed by how I got it wrong.
You tell me how I need to change
but say you'll help and make me
    strong.
I know that I can trust you,
you want what's best for me.
You prompt me to keep growing,
to be the best that I can be.

Move this mountain

Lord please move this mountain from in
front of me,
it's so wide and so high, it's all I can see.
I don't know how to conquer it all on my
own –
I'm tired, I can't cope and I want to go
home.
I've gone round in circles thinking it
through,
I'm completely stuck – I need help from
you.
You're all powerful – it'll move if that is your
will.
Otherwise, give me the strength if I must
climb up that hill.
I don't understand why things happen as
they do
but that doesn't matter, I have faith and
trust in you.

Be kind

Be kind to them –
remember I made them that way.
Be kind to them –
you can't see but it's been a bad
    day.
Be kind to them –
you don't know what's gone before.
Be kind to them –
they're struggling and can't take
    much more.
They don't yet know me
but I'm sending you in my place.
You don't need to fix their
    problems,
just be a friendly face.
When you were like them
I was there for you,
now go and share my love,
that's all I ask of you.

Pleasing to your sight

Lord help me not to let
your light in me grow dim.
I know the truth so want to
stay far away from sin.
But it's easy for the small things
to come creeping up on me.
Lord, give me wisdom and
    discernment
so I'll always clearly see
what it is you want from me
and how I ought to act,
how to always walk in love
and distinguish lies from fact.
I don't want to be influenced
by what the world may view as
    right.
When you look upon me
I want to be pleasing to your sight.

Faithful in my promises

I am faithful in my promises,
if I've said it then it will be so.
I will choose the timing,
how and when, you will not know.
Have confidence, my plan is perfect
and there's a part in it just for you.
Each time I see your obedience
I'll trust you with more to do.

Look forward

Sometimes when I look forward
to the person I want to be
it can be a bit discouraging –
an end too far away to see.
But if I turn and look backwards
at how far I've already come,
I'm reminded of your love for me
and battles already won.

Asking for your help

I won't keep asking for your help
I know it's already given to me.
Instead I thank you in advance
for all those things I've yet to see.
I trust your ways and will follow them,
I know you always want what's best.
I can give up my struggling and striving –
through you I work from a place of a rest.

The way you work

It's amazing to see the way that you work.
When I feel like I haven't gotten anywhere
you'll give me a sign of encouragement –
someone will respond to what I have to share.
I know it's all about the bigger picture,
and everything will happen in your time,
but it comforts to know that I can spread your
    word
through every obedience of mine.

When I feel I have nothing

When I feel I have nothing
I remember I have you.
When I'm confused and lost
you'll guide my way through.
When I call out in the darkness
you'll always hear when I pray.
No matter what happens
you're with me to stay.

Help me to be still

Help me to be still, to be patient and wait,
to trust in your timing, you're never early or
    late.
Help me be quiet and listen for your voice,
to first seek your guidance when making a
    choice.
Help me find you even in the busiest day,
to always be obedient when it's not the
    easiest way.
Help me take time to be still and just be,
to remember to invite you to come talk with
    me.

I wait on you

I wait on you to speak to me,
to open my mind and help me see,
to help me look beyond this place,
to strengthen me to run my race,
to give me wisdom for what to say,
to give me love enough for each
    day.

Lord lead me

Lord lead me down the road
that you would have me travel
and guide me in the way I ought to
    turn.
I feel so far from home –
there are so many distractions
and there's so much more I know I
    need to learn.
The road just keeps on going
with many twists and turns.
I can't see where it heads or it will end
but I know I needn't worry
because you are there beside me,
my ever-present guide and my friend.

Give me patience

Please give me patience
as I slowly learn and grow.
Please give me understanding
for all I need to know.
Help me take the time
to really get to know you,
and not just spend it asking
what I'd like you to do.
Help me to always listen
even if I don't like what you say.
Help me to make you
my first and last thought of the day.
Help me to appreciate
the season that I'm in.
Help me look back with kindness
and learn from where I've been.
Help me not to want to
rush straight to the end,
but make the most of challenges
and opportunities that you send.

Meet me here

Take the time to meet me here
be quiet so you can hear my voice.
I want to speak into your heart
and guide your every choice.
Don't be consumed by your own plans,
I have things I need you to do.
So seek my guidance of what's in store
and I'll be faithful to you.

Sleep my little one

Sleep my little one
let your cares float away –
relax into slumber
at the end of the day.
Enter your dream world –
it's all you need do –
you're safe in this place
and I'll watch over you.

Fanning the flames

Like fanning the flames, each word takes
   it higher,
throwing more fuel onto the fire.
Holy Spirit work in me to extinguish the
   heat –
help me choose peace and not see it as
   defeat.
Help me choose calmness over proving
   I'm right –
remove all my anger and replace it with
   light.

Speak wisdom
from you

Lord help me to keep my mouth shut
until I can speak wisdom from you.
If others come and ask for advice
help me pray first and fully think it through.
You alone have the love and understanding,
I only see things from my point of view.
Only you can give me the right words to
    share.
Only you know what others should do.

Hold my tongue

Help me know whether to hold my tongue,
or to keep on arguing until the battle's won.
Help me know whether to stand up and fight
or quietly explain wrong from right.
Give me wisdom and discernment every time,
give me your words instead of mine.

Choose my battles

Lord, help me to choose my battles,
to know whether to speak up or to ignore.
There's so much in life that can be irritating
I don't want to live life annoyed anymore.
I start every day praying to be peaceful
but fear that I always fail the test.
Please show me what it is that's important
and help me let go of the rest.

I choose faithfulness

I choose faithfulness over fear.
I choose not to hold back but be near.
I choose to worship despite the pain.
I choose to believe I'll see the light
   again.
I choose you to guide me
rather than to find my own way.
I choose to believe in your words
rather than what others may say.

Can anything really change?

Can anything really change
if the mind remains the same,
conforming on the outside
but only to avoid the shame?
Behave the way you're told to
or you'll stand out from the crowd,
fall in with our ideas,
questioning the norm is not allowed.
But God gives strength and wisdom
to swim against the tide,
to stand up for his truths,
to not shrink back and hide.
With him you can grow and flourish,
your mind can be made new.
He will give you the desire
for what he wants you to do.

Let me see clearly

Open my eyes and let me see clearly,
show me what you want me to do.
Help me respond in the way you desire,
not led by words or emotion untrue.
Only you know the plan that goes deeper,
spread through the years, not just today.
Only you know the impact of each action,
so please guide me and show me the way.

It takes courage

It takes courage to stand apart
    from others
and declare what God has laid on
    your heart.
You might feel alone and
    deserted
but you need to keep playing
    your part.
Don't get carried away with
    emotion
but continue to check in with
    him,
let him guide you each step of
    the journey
and by staying true you will win.

Keep me in your heart

Keep me in your heart
as you go about your day,
listen to my promptings
I'll guide you the right way.
Reach out to those who are in need –
there's so many all around –
so when doubters look for proof
in you, I will be found.

Thought a fool

If I'm going to be thought a fool
then I'll be a fool for you.
Though many don't understand it
and mock the things I do.
I'd rather be thought silly
during my short life here on earth,
then when I get to heaven
I'll know I've shown my worth.

Change your focus

Change your focus and lift up your eyes –
you don't need to dwell on the world's
    fears.
Despite all his efforts, man will not change
and conflicts will continue through the
    years.
But despite all of this, you should never
    give up
but look to me to bring the world light.
I am the redeemer, the saviour of all,
I shine brightest in the darkness of night.

Create in me compassion

Create in me compassion
to help those I see in need –
to be concerned about the lives of
    others
and not consumed by my own greed.
Needs and wants are different things,
I know you'll always provide for me,
so help me be grateful for what I have
and not always wanting all I see.

The old ways are not working

The old ways are not working,
let me guide you to the new.
No more switching to autopilot,
it's time to think about what you do.
Step out from what's familiar
don't just play it safe.
Be ready for new adventures
as I lead you to a different place.

Weapon of love

Rise up and fight with the weapon of love,
a supernatural force bestowed from above.
Don't conform to the ways of this land,
dare to be different and follow God's plan.
Though some may mock and disbelieve what
    you say,
meet them with love, and for them pray.
For you were once like them – you'd strayed
    off the track.
God loves them too, help guide them back.

Pull together

In these challenging times we should all pull
    together,
we must forget our differences and all work
    as one.
Give our support and continue to lift others
and not tire of this until the battle is won.
We cannot become a group that's divided,
remember we're fighting towards the same
    end.
Let's walk in love and demonstrate God's
    goodness,
let's be the people on whom others can
    depend.

I want to see the evidence

I don't find it a pleasure
to hear you repeat the words I've said,
when I can't see that the knowledge
has moved to your heart from your
    head.
It's not enough that you know my words
if your actions don't match what you
    say –
I want to see the evidence
in how you live your life each day.

Joined in one spirit

Aren't we all joined in one spirit,
shouldn't we come together in Christ?
Didn't he save us all equally
when he paid the ultimate price?
Can't we encourage each other,
not be pulled apart by differing views?
Shouldn't we be more supportive
as we all share in the same good news?

Unending praise

Unending praise is what you deserve.
My life's purpose is to love and to serve,
to look for your guidance and follow your plan,
you alone are worthy, you're the great I Am.

Divisions forming

Such divisions forming
as people speak their mind,
rushing in with comments
about every topic that they find.
Can't everyone be a little nicer?
We might not agree, we're not all the
    same –
could we try to be more understanding
and not just seek to lay the blame?
We're all in this together
each with a different daily struggle –
perhaps if we try and help each other
we'll better manage all we've got to
    juggle.

Why do you not speak of me?

Why do you not speak of me?
Are you ashamed?
My grace is right here
ready to be claimed.
If you do not tell them
how will they know?
Without my love at death
where will they go?
I know it's not easy
standing out from the crowd,
but be bold for me
proclaim me out loud,
explain all the things
that I've done for you,
tell everyone you meet
how they can be made new.
I'm always with you,
I'll give you the strength and
    words.
Please don't stop telling
until everyone has heard.

Don't give up

Don't give up on the praise you are
    giving
though you are few, you are seen and
    heard.
It's important that you continue to
    worship,
to witness to others and spread my word.
I go with you and will be in your
    encounters,
be brave and don't fear what others may
    say.
Be proud that you're out working for me
and you'll be rewarded on judgement day.

Come together in worship

Come together in worship
draw others to join your praise,
I want to see you lift my name
and celebrate me all your days.
I don't want just one day a week
where you remember to hold
    me dear.
I want each minute of every day
where you follow and keep me
    near.

Examine your motives

Examine your motives – is your heart
true?
Are you following my will or what the
world wants from you?
Are you easily led away from the truth?
Do you accept all as fact or look for the
proof?
Mine is the way that I want you to go,
mine is the truth that I want you to
know.

Open my mind

Open my mind to endless possibility,
widen my vision of what things could be,
let my expectations not be set in stone,
help me step away from my narrow
    comfort zone.
Help me adapt and deal with the
    unknown,
help me embrace challenge and make it
    my own,
help me transition through periods of
    change,
so, no matter what happens, my calm will
    remain.

It starts
with a few

It starts with a few but will end with
    many
singing and shouting my praise.
Look to the future and don't be
    discouraged
because I'm counting down the days.
I have a plan and my kingdom will come
all on earth will be put right.
But, until that time, I'm calling my
    people
to stand up for me and fight.
Fight the injustice, fight the lies
and fight the apathy.
No matter what's going on in the world
focus your eyes on me.

We welcome you into our hearts

We welcome you here and into our
    hearts,
we're open to what you may say.
Let us feel your presence amongst us
as we offer up our worship today.
Move among us Holy Spirit
lift each of our hearts and minds.
Fill us with your love and power
and let God's glory shine.

Build me up

Build me up for the plans you have,
help me be prepared.
If I didn't know it was your idea.
I couldn't do it – I wouldn't have dared
to rely on my own understanding
and strength – it couldn't have been done.
But if it's your will and you ask me to
I know it's a fight that shall be won.

You gave me a gift

You gave me a gift
and you told me to share,
to not look at others,
contrast or compare.
So I'll focus on doing
what you ask me to do,
no matter how it's received
because I'm doing it for you.

Take heart

Take heart from the things
    you're doing
you're heading the right way,
don't be discouraged by setbacks
you can't achieve everything in
    one day.
A child takes many years to grow
and it will be the same with you,
so continue listening to my word
I'll keep showing you what to do.

Sing out my praise

Sing out my praises
come play your part,
shout out my name,
feel my joy in your heart.
Lift up your worship
to your holy king,
I'm eagerly awaiting
your offering.

Meet with you

Lord we want to meet with you
and lift your name up high,
to sing and shout your praises
to be heard by passers by.
So at this special time of year
all will come to know
that you Lord are the reason
for the celebrations that we
    throw.
You alone are the reason
for the joy found in our hearts,
as we marvel at your story
in which we now play our part
to bring your love to the world,
to help spread joy and peace
until everybody knows you
and hatred and evil cease.

Sing your song

Sing your song of joy to the Lord,
he wants to hear the praise you have for
   him.
It pleases him to hear you worship
he's gladdened when you lift your voice
   and sing.
Relax, you don't have to be word perfect
or accurate in tune and in key,
he wants your love and adoration,
it's your joy in him he wants to see.

Join the angels

Sing out and join the angels
lifting their praise to me –
focus your eyes upon heaven
and let the spirit set you free.
Don't be bound by earthly
    restrictions –
you answer to a greater name –
let your worship bring you to me
and you'll never be the same.

Always and forever

Always and forever
with us you will be,
from the very beginning
and for all eternity.
Glorious and majestic,
holy through and through,
all your ways are perfect,
honest, right and true.

You're our reason for being here

Lord you're our reason for being here,
we've come to sing your praise,
you are our creator and father,
you order all our days.
We give thanks and shout your glory,
we think on all you have done,
we lift your name above all others,
we praise you Father, Spirit and Son.

Grow me closer

Grow me closer, pull me in,
deepen my love, remove my sin,
strengthen my faith, make me your own,
change my passion so it's yours that's
    shown.
Remove my doubts, erase my fears,
comfort me through my tears.
Be the one I turn to first,
and the one who loves me at my worst.

Printed in Great Britain
by Amazon